THE EVE OF WAR

VALLEY OF THE SHADOW

ALSO BY EDWARD L. AYERS

The Oxford Book of the American South *(Co-editor)*

American Passages *(Coauthor)*

All Over the Map: Rethinking American Regions *(Co-editor)*

The Promise of the New South: Life after Reconstruction

The Edge of the South: Life in Nineteenth-Century Virginia *(Co-editor)*

Vengeance and Justice: Crime and Punishment in the
Nineteenth-Century American South

THE EVE OF WAR

VALLEY
OF THE
SHADOW

TWO COMMUNITIES IN THE
AMERICAN CIVIL WAR

EDWARD L. AYERS
ANNE S. RUBIN

W·W·Norton & Company   New York   London

The text of this book is composed in 13/15.5 Perpetua
with display set in Felix Titling.
Composition by Margaret M. Wagner
Manufacturing by The Courier Companies, Inc.
Book design and flag illustration by Margaret M. Wagner

ISBN 0-393-04604-4

W. W. Norton & Company, Inc., 500 Fifth Avenue, New York, N.Y. 10110
http://www.wwnorton.com

W. W. Norton & Company Ltd., 10 Coptic Street, London WC1A 1PU

1 2 3 4 5 6 7 8 9 0

CONTENTS

THE EVE OF WAR

VALLEY OF THE SHADOW

I
THE VALLEY

IN EARLY 1861 it seemed that every issue of the newspapers offered conflicting reports, advice, and predictions about the conflicts between the North and the South. Letters from friends and family vacillated between calm assurances and horrible foreboding. Raucous meetings fueled passions. People debated hidden implications of politicians' speeches and pronouncements. Some people boasted of what they would do if the conflict came to blows, while others remained quiet and apprehensive. Meanwhile, woven among the great national events, the occurrences and crises of daily life in mid-nineteenth-century America unfolded: childbirth and death, floods and fires, revivals and crime sprees, prosperity and poverty.

People gathered in a Pennsylvania town to hear a speech much like others being delivered across the country, a speech filled with disbelief: "Three months ago the domain of the United States extended from Maine to Florida, from the Atlantic to the Pacific; now, it stops far short of the gulf of Mexico. Three months ago 'the Stars and Stripes' waved over the forts at Pensacola, over Moultrie and Pinkney in Charleston harbor, an honored ensign, a shield to its friends, but a terror to its foes.——Now, that glorious banner whose stars have so often risen upon the night of humanity, as a beacon of hope to the oppressed, the world over, is lowered amid the howlings of Southern mobs, and trampled in the dust, with every mark of indignity." The Northern states were "seized with a military frenzy. New companies are being formed and armed. The mechanic rushes from his shop, the merchant from his store and the professional man from his office to fill up the ranks. There is a growing thirst for military

Soldiers would soon be fighting in formerly peaceful towns.

fame, and an impatience of restraint or delay. Washington city is
full of armed men. Pennsylvania Avenue is bristling with bayo-
nets, and the neighing of war steeds, and the rumbling of cannon
wagons, drown the noise and din of the trade and business of the
city. The very atmosphere about us is ladened with the noise of
preparation."

In a Virginia county not far to the south, a young man agonized over such events in a letter: " We seem to be on the very eve of Civil War—upon the very brink of destruction. It seems that the prosperity of America is about to end. Her sun seems to be setting in clouds and darkness—ruin—ruin—ruin! stares us in the face. But I have never believed that this union is to be dissolved; and I do not believe it now." The United States was too great to die at its own hand. "We have become the wonder and pride of the world and now shall we become a 'proverb and a reproach' a scorn and a bye-word? Never! Never!" This young man echoed the sense of loss expressed in the Pennsylvania speech. "I do not believe that Providence has raised up this nation to such greatness and glory, to throw it away." Within months, this advocate of the Union would be fighting—and dying—for the Confederacy.

These complicated emotions played themselves out in every county, town, and city in the United States. The crisis of the Union brought struggles within people's hearts, within their homes and communities, long before it brought struggles on the battlefield. To understand the coming of the Civil War, then, we need to pick up the story before Fort Sumter and to carry it deeper than national events. We need to understand both the advocates of conflict and those who sought to avoid it regardless of the cost. We need to understand the communities people fought to defend, the institutions that held them together and drove them apart.

To achieve that understanding, the Valley of the Shadow Project explores two counties, one in the North and one in the South. The anguished speech that opened this essay came from Franklin County, Pennsylvania; the letter from Augusta County, Virginia.

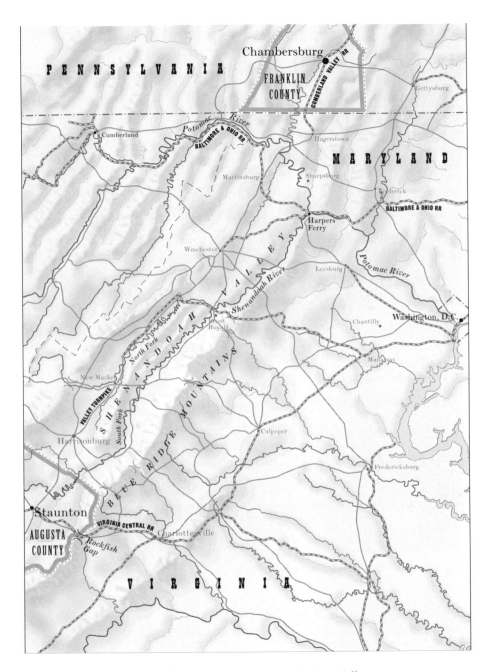

Between Franklin and Augusta lay the Great Valley.

Both of those counties lie in the Great Valley that stretches diagonally from Pennsylvania to Georgia. Franklin and Augusta, like the rest of the United States in the late 1850s and early 1860s, wrestled with the meanings and repercussions of events in Kansas, Harper's Ferry, Charleston, and Washington. The people of Augusta and Franklin, like so many people in the young nation, found themselves hating people who lived not far away, spoke the same language, worshiped at the same churches, and claimed the same political legacy and Founding Fathers. Augusta and Franklin, like characters in a story, are individuals with their own personalities, struggles, and hopes. But, also like characters in a story, their experiences were not unique; they resonated with those of many other places.

The Great Valley, formed by the congruence of the Cumberland River Valley in Pennsylvania and the Shenandoah River Valley in Virginia, was bounded on the west by the imposing Allegheny Mountains and on the east by the gentler Blue Ridge. For thousands of years, the valley had been a home for various nations of American Indians, a broad avenue of rolling land, sparkling rivers, dense forests, and limitless game. Native Americans in the southern part of the valley called their land *Shenandoah*, or "Daughter of the Stars."

The Valley held rich farm land and striking vistas.

The eighteenth century brought new kinds of people to this valley, people who displaced those who had first named the rivers and mountains. Settlers from England, Germany, Scotland, and Ireland pushed into the valley. The land was rich, the climate healthy, and the travel easy, so settlers often bypassed areas closer to the eastern coast and moved directly to the

Churches were prominent parts of the landscape in both counties.

Shenandoah and the Cumberland. The settlers barely paused in the cities of Philadelphia and Baltimore before they came to the valley, fanning out to the north and south. Some pushed all the way into the Carolinas and Georgia, often taking slaves with them, while others moved up into New York, looking for good land or likely places for mills and towns that had not already been taken.

Augusta and Franklin occupied key places about two hundred miles apart on the Great Valley Road. A steady stream of settlers passed through on their way to newer, rawer, and more remote communities; thousands, however, chose to stay in Franklin and Augusta. Those counties became prosperous farming communities dotted by churches, mills, schools, and towns. The two counties did not nurture large cities, but rather grew as so many American communities did, steadily and unspectacularly. Like those other places, too, both Augusta and Franklin were deceptively simple, their complexities of kin, race, gender, class, religion, generation, and party hidden from the casual observer.

By 1860, then, Franklin and Augusta were thriving communities. In both places, railroads had arrived in the last few years, tying Staunton (pronounced "stanton," the *u* silent), the county

Staunton in 1857

seat for Augusta County, and Chambersburg, the county seat for Franklin, to a burgeoning national network of rail lines and telegraph lines. Rich farms grew grain and livestock, small factories produced for the local market, and newspapers jostled for customers. Augusta and Franklin touched one another through marriage, trade, and circumstance; more than a few families in each county shared names with those in the other. Franklin had considerably more people than Augusta—about forty-two thousand to twenty-eight thousand—but Augusta County was physically larger. Franklin County, like other Pennsylvania and Northern counties, was divided into townships and peppered with villages. Augusta County, like other Virginia and Southern counties, possessed a more dispersed population, gathered on farms and plantations. Both Franklin and Augusta contained a number of smaller towns that vied with one another and with Staunton and Chambersburg for trade and pride. Both counties boasted a town named Waynesboro, after General Anthony Wayne of the Revolution.

No two places could be entirely characteristic of either the North or the South, but the counties we focus on in the Valley Project were by no means unusual. Farm size, property values, and population in both counties were not unlike those of hundreds of other counties in their regions, as were the number and type of manufacturing establishments, churches, and political parties. The concentration on grains and livestock rather than cotton made Augusta farms typical of much of the South. The proportion of slaves in Augusta was similar to that of most counties in the South, other than those in the Tidewater of Virginia, the rice islands of South Carolina, and the cotton belt of the Deep South.

Despite the many similarities and connections between Franklin and Augusta, slavery stood as the defining difference between the two counties. Although representatives from the Valley had expressed serious misgivings in the 1830s about the effects of slavery on white society, a growing number of influen-

Slave trading was not an unusual sight in the valley of Virginia.

tial farmers and townsmen in Augusta bought into slavery, literally and figuratively. The African-American population of the county stabilized at about a fifth of the whole, with more than five thousand slaves and nearly six hundred free blacks in 1860, their numbers growing slightly over the previous decade despite the sale of considerable numbers of slaves in the 1850s. Slaves tended wheat fields, apple orchards, and shops; they also labored side by side with white artisans. Several hundred free blacks lived on the boundary of slavery and freedom, sometimes buying a husband or wife from slavery, sometimes acquiring a small house or farm.

Franklin County also contained a considerable free black population, largely the product of Pennsylvania's emancipation several decades earlier. Because Virginia lay only five miles from Franklin's southern border, across a narrow stretch of Maryland, runaway slaves from the South who escaped up the valley often came through Franklin on the Underground Railroad. Most run-

Slaves frequently sought escape.

$100 REWARD!

I will give the above reward for a runa-

way named LEWIS, belonging to the estate of Joseph Thompson, dec'd., if he is apprehended out of State of Virginia, or $50 if apprehended in this State, provided he is delivered to me or secured in jail so that I get him.

LEWIS ran off in the month of September last, from Thomas G. Marshall, who resides near Farrowsville, in Fauquier County, and to whom he was hired for 1854. He has many acquaintances and connexions in the neighborhood of White Ridge, in Fauquier County, where he was raised, and is probably lurking in that vicinity, or he may have obtained employment in Loudoun county as a free man.

Lewis is about 5 feet 11 inches high, of black complexion, has good teeth, inclined to be spare, but is well made and likely. He is about 25 years old.

JOHN P. PHILIPS,

Administrator of Joseph Thompson, dec'd.

Warrenton, Va.

aways kept moving farther north, but others settled in Franklin. Churches and schools operated by and for black people appeared throughout the county. Despite these symbols of black aspiration and achievement, many whites in Franklin County had little use or toleration for the African Americans in their midst. One of the two local newspapers dripped with contempt for all black people and agreed with the white South that slavery was the proper place for those with dark skins, even as the other paper approvingly quoted Abraham Lincoln's attacks on slavery.

The sectional crisis of the late 1850s and early 1860s brought the divisions within each county to the surface. Augusta County had long been a stronghold of Unionism, and in 1861 virtually every white man voted for convention delegates who opposed immediate secession. Franklin County had long contained Democrats who expressed sympathy for the white South. When the moment of crisis came, however, these divisions were quickly—if temporarily—pasted over. The men of Augusta and the men of Franklin, encouraged by their wives and daughters, aligned with their states and went off to fight one another.

No one could foresee the carnage that lay ahead. Soldiers from the two counties would confront one another at many of the major battles of the eastern theater. Both Chambersburg and Staunton would occupy critical strategic locations in the war and see thousands of troops, repeated invasions, and widespread destruction. Both communities would serve as recruiting posts, hospital bases, and supply depots, their populations doubling during the war years. Chambersburg, only thirty miles from Gettysburg, would watch over one hundred thousand soldiers pass through as Robert E. Lee used the town both for preparation and for escape at the crucial battle in the North. A general

Battles tore at the Valley from the early days of the war until the end.

from Staunton would lead a seventeen-mile-long wagon train of wounded Confederates through Chambersburg on the way back to Virginia. A year later, in 1864, as Union troops closed in on Staunton, Confederates retaliating for the destruction of towns in the Valley of Virginia would burn Chambersburg to the ground.

These are the complicated places you may explore in the *Valley of the Shadow*, the dramas of common people confronted with uncommon choices. In the late 1850s and early 1860s the horrible events that would sweep over Augusta and Franklin lay in the unknowable—indeed, unimaginable—future. People could not know the consequences of their actions in these days of intoxicating purpose and bluster. African Americans could not know that their freedom lay only a few years away. In the years since the Civil War these events have lost none of their grip on us. In the *Valley of the Shadow*, you can find your own answers to the questions about the Civil War that have haunted Americans since 1861.

II
DIGITAL HISTORY

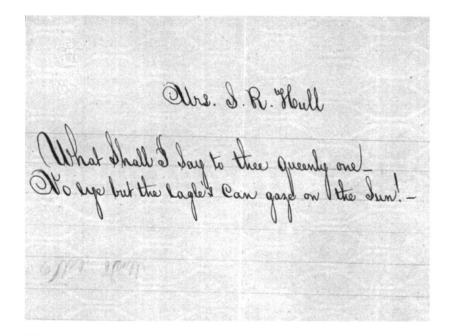

Mrs. S. R. Hull

What shall I say to thee queenly one—
No eye but the eagle's can gaze on the sun!—

MOST ACCOUNTS of the Civil War, understandably enough, tend to focus on national events. Those interpretations offer the words of Abraham Lincoln and other political leaders at the vortex of the conflict, making momentous decisions. They trace a series of events that seem to lead inexorably to war. While these decisions are central to understanding the war—and are available in the Valley Project—they do not convey a full sense of the way the average person experienced the late 1850s and early 1860s.

Whether they lived in the North or the South, whether they were black or white, people did not know they were living through a series of crises that would bring on a war that would kill 625,000 Americans, a proportion of the population equal to over 5 million people today.

It is much easier to gather documents from official papers and a few national newspapers than it is to do the sort of research represented in the Valley of the Shadow Project. Almost all the materials before you have never been studied by historians before, representing as they do the stuff of everyday life in everyday places. It is harder, ironically, to study the commonplace than it is to study the "historic," yet there is a kind of healthy discipline that comes from limiting ourselves to what we can learn about two places. There is a kind of rigor that comes from valuing and examining every piece of evidence. There is a kind of historical knowledge that comes from recognizing that the people of the nineteenth-century United States were as complicated, and as limited in their understanding, as we are today. We need not abandon the study of great people, of course; but we can benefit from thinking about average Americans, people reacting to events not of their making.

The Valley of the Shadow Project is the product of an enormous labor on the part of dozens of people at the University of Virginia. Over the last several years, those people, most of them historians or historians in training, have transcribed the names of every free man, woman, and child in the two counties from everything from church records to registries of free blacks. They have indexed and selected for transcription many hundreds of newspaper articles, making it possible to search for any individual who was ever mentioned in the papers for any reason. They

A page from the manufacturing census, one of several such large documents transcribed for the Valley Project.

have painstakingly connected names on the population, agricul-
tural, and slave censuses with maps from the period. They have
searched in libraries, archives, schools, churches, and homes
throughout two states and the nation's capital for letters, diaries,
and photographs from the two communities. They have taken
hundreds of photographs of extant buildings and recorded music
from the period. They have held public meetings to solicit materials and to involve latter-day residents of the communities in the
research.

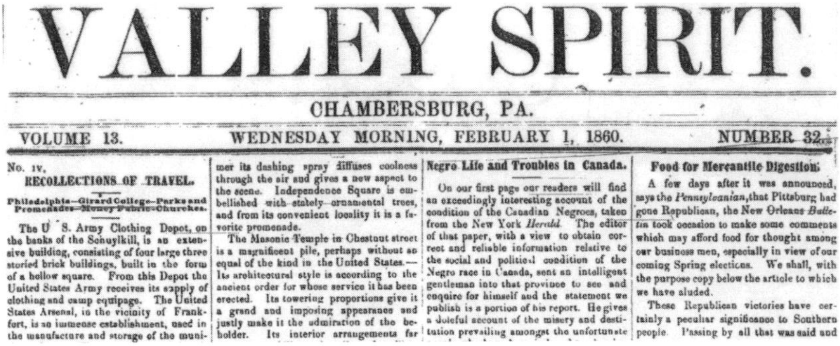

VALLEY SPIRIT.

CHAMBERSBURG, PA.

VOLUME 13. WEDNESDAY MORNING, FEBRUARY 1, 1860. NUMBER 32.

No. IV.

RECOLLECTIONS OF TRAVEL.

Philadelphia—Girard College—Parks and Promenades—Money Public—Churches.

The U. S. Army Clothing Depot, on the banks of the Schuylkill, is an extensive building, consisting of four large three storied brick buildings, built in the form of a hollow square. From this Depot the United States Army receives its supply of clothing and camp equipage. The United States Arsenal, in the vicinity of Frankfort, is an immense establishment, used in the manufacture and storage of the muni-

mer its dashing spray diffuses coolness through the air and gives a new aspect to the scene. Independence Square is embellished with stately ornamental trees, and from its convenient locality it is a favorite promenade.

The Masonic Temple in Chestnut street is a magnificent pile, perhaps without an equal of the kind in the United States.—Its architectural style is according to the ancient order for whose service it has been erected. Its towering proportions give it a grand and imposing appearance and justly make it the admiration of the beholder. Its interior arrangements far

Negro Life and Troubles in Canada.

On our first page our readers will find an exceedingly interesting account of the condition of the Canadian Negroes, taken from the New York *Herald*. The editor of that paper, with a view to obtain correct and reliable information relative to the social and political condition of the Negro race in Canada, sent an intelligent gentleman into that province to see and enquire for himself and the statement we publish is a portion of his report. He gives a doleful account of the misery and destitution prevailing amongst the unfortunate

Food for Mercantile Digestion.

A few days after it was announced, says the *Pennsylvanian*, that Pittsburg had gone Republican, the New Orleans *Bulletin* took occasion to make some comments which may afford food for thought among our business men, especially in view of our coming Spring elections. We shall, with the purpose copy below the article to which we have aluded.

These Republican victories have certainly a peculiar significance to Southern people. Passing by all that was said and

Newspapers form a critical part of the Valley Project.

The project began in 1991, when the University of Virginia received an invitation from the IBM Corporation to conceive of effective new uses for powerful networked computers. The result was the Institute for Advanced Technology in the Humanities. The Valley of the Shadow Project, one of the two pilot projects for the new institute, attempted to make the raw materials of history available in a new form. The acquisition, digitizing, and cataloging of the census and newspapers began without a clear sense of how they might be held together and shared with others, but the advent of the World Wide Web soon provided one means. Early versions of the project have appeared on the Web in the years since, growing larger and more complex with each iteration, benefiting from the suggestions of many users. We have drawn essential support from the University of Virginia and the National Endowment for the Humanities.

While the Web has evolved more rapidly than anyone could have imagined at the beginning of the 1990s, its limited capabilities have led us to use CD-ROM, a medium that allows for a far richer and more fluid environment than the Web. Our Web site offers access to the large databases on which the project is based, along with a place to share ideas and to offer additional research materials, but the CD contains a far more developed set of evidence and tools than the Web can currently handle well. We have provided considerable help to those exploring this archive: the narrative in this companion book; powerful tools for searching and gathering evidence on the CD and on the Web; background information on sources, people, and events at convenient points throughout the electronic archive.

Each feature of the CD adds a rich overlay. The photographs and images connect us with the look and feel of the past, its proportions and textures, its similarities to our own time as well as the differences. The music reminds us of the emotional range of

The opening page of the Valley web site.

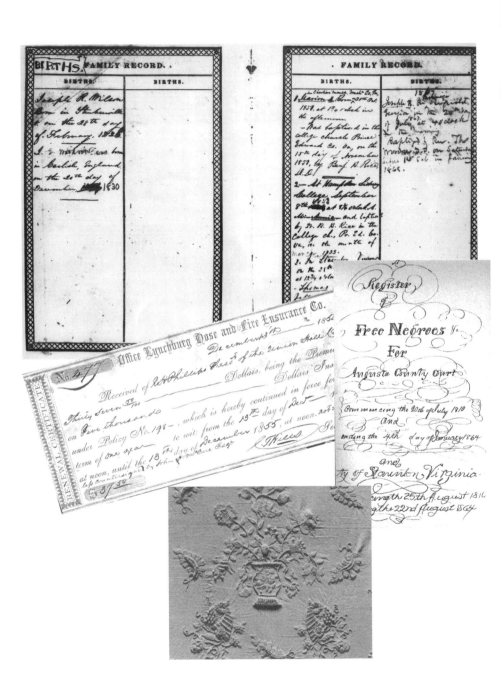

the past, of the humanity of the people who lived in the nine-teenth century. The interactive maps serve both as guides to the patterns of family, congregation, class, race, and party and as reminders of how much nineteenth-century life depended on the landscape, on the importance of rivers, soils, slopes, roads, and railroads. The timelines allow us to orient ourselves in par-allel streams of events and processes. The discussions of docu-ments alert us to the possibilities and limitations of each kind of evidence, telling us where each came from, who gathered it and why, how it can be used, what it can and cannot reveal.

You can follow many pathways through the Valley Project. The easiest and most familiar kind of exploration is simply reading newspapers, diaries, and letters. The transcription and grouping of those documents make them much easier to use than they would otherwise be. Rather than having to read through months of newspapers for one or two mentions of a person, you can quickly find those instances and then build on them with other kinds of evidence. To find the two quotes that began this essay, for example, you could learn from the timelines when the sec-tional crisis had built to a feverish stage but had yet to become resolved into conflict between a fully formed Confederacy and Union. In the newspapers and personal papers in January and February of 1861 you would find dozens of speeches, represent-ing every shade of political opinion, along with memoirs and let-ters from Augusta and Franklin, reflecting both wild enthusiasm and profound doubt. Earlier or later months would reveal dif-ferent configurations of emotion, loyalty, and conviction.

The Valley Project offers many kinds of stories that have little to do with politics and public events. You can follow hints to weave together intimate stories of family life. On the back of a quilt in the "Material Culture" section of the CD, for instance, you will find these words stitched into one panel: "Presented to Eugenia E. Bumgardner by her Mother on the 15 anniversary of her birth 1855." We know from the description of the quilt that Eugenia's mother was Melinda Bumgardner. If we search for the Bumgardners in the census, we find the mother but not the daughter. Since we know from the discussion of the census that four years passed between the time the quilt was made and the census was taken, we might fear that Eugenia died as a young woman. Searching the newspaper for Eugenia Bumgardner, how-

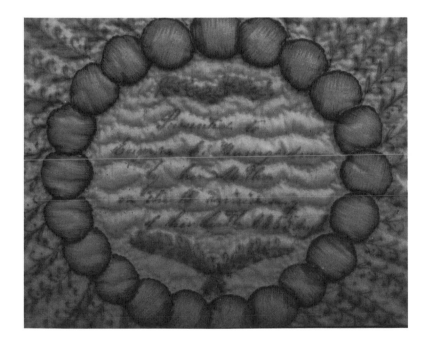

A detail from the quilt made by Melinda Bumgardner.

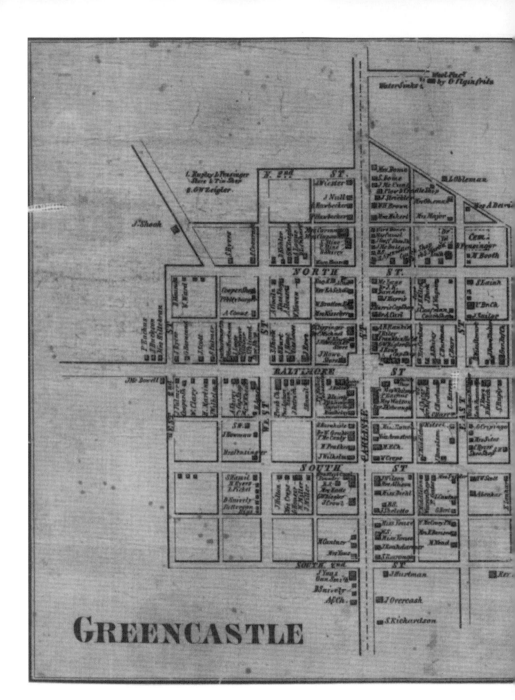

GREENCASTLE

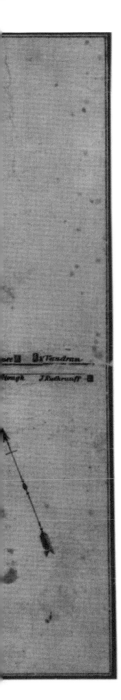

ever, turns up a wedding announcement instead, when she married Archibald Sproul in 1859. Searching then for the Sproul family, we find the nineteen-year-old wife and her slightly older husband. We also find his brother, mother, and sisters living in a nearby home, along with evidence of their considerable wealth and slaveholding. Spinning out our researches from this discovery, we can learn about unmarried women in the newspapers, the division of slaves and land by well-to-do families, the interconnections among elite families, and even the political divisions in the county. On the next CDs, you will be able to trace the Bumgardners and the Sprouls into the war and then into a bracing postwar world.

You might wish instead to explore a community from the ground up. We have gone to considerable trouble to link residential maps from the mid-nineteenth century with other records. Since these maps included only property holders, they leave out residents who owned no property. But, as with much of the evidence in the Valley Project, you can read between the lines to learn more about poorer people. By locating whites who owned property in Antrim township in Franklin County, for example, and examining their names on the census, you can see that

Many free blacks lived in the Greencastle area of Franklin County.

African-American families lived among them, locating the area where black people lived in a way that would be impossible otherwise. Once you see that Greencastle held quite a sizable black population, you might explore the differences and similarities between African-American life in Franklin and in Augusta. You could create profiles of the free black population of both counties, examining aspects such as average wealth or family size. You might read representations of African Americans in the four newspapers transcribed here, which in turn could lead you to explore runaway slaves from Augusta and the operation of the Underground Railroad in Franklin. Every strand leads to another strand; every story leads to another.

If history is about bringing our ideas and received wisdom into contact with evidence of the past, it is also about bringing our conclusions into contact with those of others who look at the same evidence. History is written to be shared. We need to test and improve our ideas by comparing them with those of other researchers. The Valley Web site is devoted to that sharing, and we encourage you to let others know what you find in the Valley archive. Whether you write a paragraph or an essay of fifty pages, your work is more interesting if it becomes the basis for a conversation. Patterns lie latent in the digital data we provide, but they become history only when people translate them into stories and arguments.

And there will be arguments. The Valley Project demonstrates what historians have long known: the evidence does not speak for itself, nor does it tell only one story. People have always disagreed about the war's causes and outcome. Right up to the day of secession, editors, correspondents, and citizens filled the newspapers with invective and persuasion, with doubt and fear,

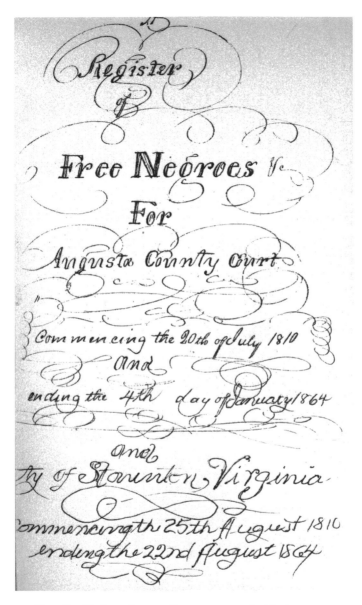

*Many free blacks in Augusta County registered with the court to
protect their freedom and their property.*

arguing with their neighbors as well as with far-away enemies. During the war that followed, people on both sides continually reinterpreted the causes of the conflict, forgetting or disavowing much they had said before April 1861.

Over the generations since, historians have wrestled with virtually every facet of the war's origins, fighting, and outcome. For many decades, the North and the South held to their own, mutually exclusive interpretations of the war, blaming the other side for the deaths of their brothers, fathers, and grandfathers. After World War I, leading historians began to question the wisdom and necessity of the Civil War. They established their arguments on what they saw as a professional, even scientific, basis, locating the bloodshed in the mistakes of a "blundering generation." After World War II, however, the country's most prominent historians argued that the war's origins lay squarely in slavery and thus could not be avoided. In this interpretation, the North appeared as a modern society in fundamental conflict with the South's archaic system of slavery. Slavery was not merely a moral affront but also an obstacle to progress.

Today, many shadings of interpretation compete with another to explain the path to war. Some historians emphasize political parties and individual decisions, while others emphasize broader forces beyond the control of individuals; some stress the abolitionists, while others stress a general anti-Southern feeling in the North; some stress Southern belligerence, while others stress the North's growing power and confidence. No one gains a hearing these days for a simple economic interpretation in which tariffs and taxes drive the conflict, and no one speaks of the fanaticism of the abolitionists. Historians look instead to deeper, more fundamental kinds of conflicts and struggles.

The war took its toll on family life. This refugee family leaves a war area with belongings loaded on a wagon.

A general consensus seems to have emerged in our public culture. That consensus appears in the popularity of works such as Ken Burns's television epic *The Civil War*, best-selling novels such as Michael Shaara's *The Killer Angels*, and prize-winning and influential histories such as James McPherson's *Battle Cry of Freedom* and Gary Wills's *Lincoln at Gettysburg*. The consensus in those works is that serious conflict between the North and the South was bound to occur because the two societies were organized on different principles, that the North gradually awakened to the inhumanity of slavery over the course of the war, and that Abraham Lincoln both embodied and led the moral growth of the Union. By war's end in 1865, it appears from these accounts, the nation had been refounded on a more equitable and durable foundation. This is the interpretation that is written into American textbooks, and taught in the schools, even in the South. In

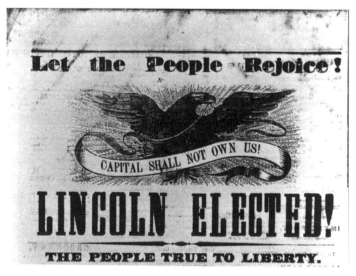

A Northern view of Lincoln's election.

the Valley Project you can test this consensus view and accept, reject, or modify it.

The information on daily life, economy, household, and race relations on this CD lets you measure the difference that slavery made. You can see how deeply and in what directions the loyalties ran for Augusta whites and how they changed over time. You can see how Northerners balanced their devotion to Union with their desire for peace. You can see how many whites in Franklin expressed sympathy for slavery and slaveholders and how many thought slavery was wrong and should be destroyed. You can see how race relations differed in the North and the South on the eve of the war. You can see how many people at the time thought warfare between North and South was impending and how many were certain that some compromise could and would be reached.

The Valley Project does not push any particular interpretation; there is raw material here that, if selectively quoted, could support many arguments. The project, however, does encourage a particular *kind* of history and understanding. It includes as many people as possible and takes all their motives seriously. It recognizes that there were more than two sides to the Civil War, that blacks and whites, rich and poor, Democrats and Republicans, and men and women saw things differently. The project invites you to reconstruct the moral logic of motives and examine how that logic bent and buckled under stress, how it faded and then reasserted itself.

III
THE IMPENDING CRISIS

 *THE EVENTS* reflected in the Valley Project were, of course, part
of a much larger story. It might be useful to pick up that story
about five years before the documents of the Valley Project begin
and to remind ourselves of the sequence of events on the national stage. In retrospect, we can see how a series of broken trusts,
broken bonds, and broken promises led to the American Civil
War. While these political events certainly attracted enormous
attention and created growing animosity between the North and

the South, we must not forget, however, that the people of the time had no idea that the Civil War was awaiting them. Indeed, many people throughout the country believed such a conflict impossible and, therefore, talked and acted recklessly. No one could have foreseen that their words and deeds would end in bloodshed—and freedom.

The Kansas-Nebraska Act of 1854, for example, had been intended by its sponsor, Senator Stephen A. Douglas of Illinois,

Stephen Douglass,
Senator from
Illinois.

to bring the long-brewing conflict over slavery to an end. Douglas had great faith in "popular sovereignty," in letting settlers decide for themselves what kind of society they would create, unencumbered by outsiders, including the national government. Certain that slavery could not survive in the vast Northern territories, Douglas was content to let slavery die a quiet death there. Instead of endangering the Union by permitting Congress to fight over slavery once again, Douglas reasoned, he would let geography, climate, and the interests of settlers bring slavery to a "natural" end.

Most of the people who moved to Kansas, from both the North and the South, moved there simply to get land and put up towns. In the distrustful, even desperate, political environment of 1855, however, outsiders dared not let the Kansas territory alone for fear their opponents would refuse to let history follow what they considered its natural course. Both Northern and Southern partisans proclaimed their determination to fill the territory with settlers of their own political persuasion. "Come on, then, Gentlemen of the slave States," New York's Senator William H. Seward proclaimed soon after the Kansas-Nebraska Act passed. "Since there is no escaping your challenge, I accept it in behalf of the cause of freedom. We will engage in competition for the virgin soil of Kansas, and God give the victory to the side which is stronger in numbers as it is in right." An Augusta County newspaper warned Southerners not to take the bait: "the scheme is suicidal, because it urges citizens of Virginia to emigrate from the State, when we have no surplus population to spare. . . . We cannot even spare the negroes to send to Kansas, as the present high price of labor sufficiently proves. . . . It is useless for the South to enter into a contest of this kind with the free

States. The advantages are all with them, and we shall surely be beaten. Far better plant ourselves on the Constitution and be content to remain there. When that fails to protect our rights, all will be lost, and we must resort to other modes of redress."

The abolitionist press, building on over thirty years of experience with shaping public opinion, created the impression that the antislavery settlers constituted a formidable foe. Proslavery advocates across the Kansas border in Missouri decided, therefore, that they had to fight to keep their property—human and otherwise—from being threatened by what they saw as Yankee invaders. On election day, these Missourians flooded across the border to vote in support of the proslavery candidates for the territorial legislature. This inflammatory action by the "border ruffians," as the northern press quickly labeled them, was not necessary: Southerners accounted for six of every ten men set-

People in the East paid close attention to the events in Kansas.

tled in Kansas by 1855. But slaveholders wanted to take no chances. In control of the territorial legislature in Lecompton, these proslavery men passed a series of aggressive laws against free-soil advocates. Forbidding antislavery men to serve on juries or to hold office, the legislature also decreed the death penalty for any person who assisted a fugitive slave.

Supporters of free soil back in New England and New York, including church congregations, sent rifles to Kansas to arm what they saw as the side of righteousness. Southerners, in turn, organized an expedition to reinforce their comrades. Not surprisingly, this volatile situation soon exploded into violence. On May 21, 1856, a group of slave-state supporters, angered by free-state newspapers and rumors of military drills by their opponents, marched into the free-soil stronghold of Lawrence, threw printing presses into the creek, and fired cannon at the Free State Hotel, which, they believed, had been established as a free-soil fortress. The cannon shot proving inadequate, the slave-state men burned the hotel to the ground. Free-soilers quickly labeled the episode the "Sack of Lawrence."

Repercussions were not long in coming. In the nation's capital the very next day, young Representative Preston Brooks of South Carolina searched out Senator Charles Sumner of Massachusetts. Sumner had delivered a series of bitter speeches against slavery, the last one focusing on the "crime against Kansas." Sumner attacked Brooks's relative and fellow South Carolinian, the elderly Senator Andrew P. Butler, for taking "the harlot, slavery" as his "mistress" and ridiculed the old man for spitting when he talked. Brooks felt that he had no choice but to defend the honor of his family and his state. He demonstrated his contempt for Sumner by striking him repeatedly about the head with a heavy rubber

Preston Brooks'
attack on
Charles Sumner
(right) polar-
ized the nation.

cane. Sumner, seated at a Senate desk screwed to the floor, ripped the chair from its moorings as he tried to rise.

In Franklin County, readers of the Democratic newspaper *The Valley Spirit* received conflicting reports on the seriousness of Sumner's injuries. The first dispatch suggested that "Mr. Sumner has two severe but not dangerous wounds on the head," but the second dispatch offered more graphic and more disturbing descriptions: "Mr. Sumner's wounds bled profusely. His physicians say they are the most serious flesh wounds they ever saw on a man's head." The senator was not to return to his seat for two and a half years, the victim of psychosomatic shock. The empty seat became a symbol in the North of Southern brutality, even insanity, on the slavery issue; the incident became a symbol in the South of the only sort of response the North would respect. Supporters from across the South sent Representative Brooks an abundance of new canes to replace the one he had broken on their behalf.

The day after Brooks's attack on Sumner an event in Kansas escalated the already volatile conflict. The episode swirled around one John Brown, a free-soil emigrant to Kansas. Brown was fifty-six years old, a man who had failed in twenty different

businesses in six states. He had been a supporter of abolitionism since 1834 and followed five of his sons to Kansas in 1855. There, he became furious at the proslavery forces and entered into the fight against them. Brown accompanied a group of free-staters to defend Lawrence, but they heard of the hotel's

John Brown burst into prominence in Kansas.

destruction before they arrived. Brown persuaded four of his sons and a son-in-law, along with two other men, to exact revenge for the defeat. Sharpening their broadswords to razor-like edges, the band set out for Pottawatomie Creek. There, acting in the name of the "Army of the North," they took five men from three houses and, after questioning them, split open their skulls. The men who were killed had been associated in some way with the territorial district court, but no one was, or is, sure of Brown's precise motives. He was never punished for the killings, though it was widely reported that he was responsible.

In the wake of the Sack of Lawrence, the caning of Sumner, and the "Pottawatomie Massacre"—exploding in just a three-day period in May 1856—the territory became known as "Bleeding Kansas." Though many Kansans wanted only to be left alone, and much bloodshed had little to do directly with slavery, the territory became the symbolic battleground for the entire nation. Both sides felt themselves a part of something larger than themselves. Far more than ever before, the North as a whole turned against the South as a whole. Both sides saw what they considered the worst in the other: abolitionism in the North and lawlessness in the South. The Kansas dispute showed that the North and the South could not peacefully coexist without a clear boundary separating them.

In one Northern state after another, voters began to listen to what the new Republican Party had to say and what it had to offer. Republicans argued that Southern slaveholders posed the greatest and most immediate threat to the free citizens of the North. The dangers that the precursors to the Republicans had seen in immigrants, the pope, and alcohol, leaders of the new party urged, should be addressed only after the immediate threat of the South had been answered. The border ruffians, the caning of Sumner, and the Sack of Lawrence could not have been more useful to the nascent Republican Party if it had orchestrated those events itself. Each clash in Kansas bolstered the fundamental argument of the party: the white South could not be trusted. The slaveholders, the Republicans charged, would stop at nothing to get their way, whether that involved stealing elections, destroying presses, burning towns, or bludgeoning Northern congressmen who dared disagree with them. The Republican Party witnessed the infusion of new energy and new men, virtually overnight.

The Democrats, on the other hand, grew dispirited and fractured. President Franklin Pierce seemed incapable of leadership, many in his party decided, and they set about looking for a new candidate for the fall election. Stephen Douglas was, by a considerable margin, the most talented and energetic leading Democrat, but many voters blamed him for the debacle in Kansas. The Democrats needed someone who had not been tarnished by the events of the preceding two years and so they turned to James Buchanan who, as minister to England, had conveniently been out of the country during the entire Kansas mess. He was also from Pennsylvania, a key state. In fact, Buchanan had been born in Franklin County, which still counted him as a native son. The prominent politician kept in touch with old friends in his hometown. The Democratic Party in Franklin made little effort to contain its hyperbole when it appeared that Buchanan would become president. "Every dweller on the soil of old Franklin has at all times something to remind him of JAMES BUCHANAN. Every evening the sun goes down behind the mountain at whose rugged base Pennsylvania's favorite son was born. . . . As that mountain stands out upon the glorious landscape spread around us—distinct, majestic, sublime, and unapproachable in grandeur—so stands out JAMES BUCHANAN among the statesmen of the Union, without a rival to come near him."

The Republicans, though growing stronger every day, turned to an unlikely candidate in 1856, John C. Frémont, a young self-made man who had achieved fame as an explorer of the west in the 1840s and 1850s. He had taken almost no public positions and accumulated almost no political experience—and what experience he did have was as a Democrat. The Republicans thought they had found just the sort of vague candidate who would give few potential voters a reason to vote against him.

John C. Frémont, Republican candidate for President in 1856.

The new party tended to be antislavery but not necessarily pro-black; Republicans avoided talking about race at all if they could help it. What they did talk about was the goodness of the North: its free labor, its free speech, its free soil. The North, they argued, was everything the South was not, a place where hard-working white men could build a life for their families free from the threat of arrogant, powerful, and greedy slaveholders. The Republicans identified something they called the "Slave Power," a conspiracy of the most powerful slaveholders to control the federal government and, therefore, the west and the future. Republicans saw everything from the Constitution's three-fifths clause to the Missouri Compromise to the war with Mexico to the bloodshed in Kansas as the fruit of the Slave Power. How else to explain the long list of Southern victories at a time when the North grew more populous and wealthy? As the Republican paper in Chambersburg put it, "We shall not hesitate to expose and denounce every treacherous attempt that may be made by the Slave power, North or South, to carry out the infamous outrages which have been successfully inaugurated in that Territory."

On election day in 1856, 83 percent of the eligible voting men in the country went to the polls, one of the highest turnouts of the era. Buchanan won all of the South except Maryland, which, along with five Northern states, went for the Nativist Party candidate, Millard Fillmore; Frémont won the rest of the Northern states. Buchanan received only 45 percent of the popular vote, while Frémont won 33 percent and Fillmore, 22 percent. A few thousand votes in a few states and Buchanan would not have been elected. The Democrats had won, but were filled with anxiety; the Republicans had lost, but they were filled with confidence. It was clear to everyone that the American political system was in

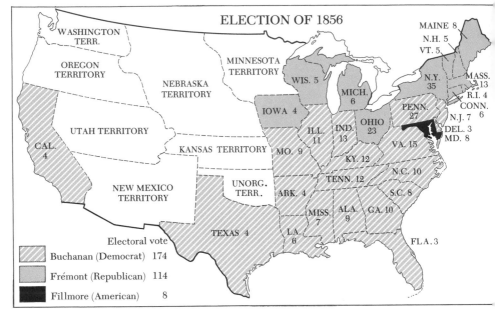

The election of 1856 showed the distance that separated North and South.

flux. No sooner was the 1856 election over than political leaders and editors began planning for the next one.

Although James Buchanan faced a challenging situation when he took office in 1857, observers of all political persuasions believed that the new president had it within his power to restore the Democrats in both the North and the South. His party, after all, still controlled both houses of Congress and the Supreme Court as well as the presidency. The Republicans, moreover, had drawn much of their power from the chaos in Kansas; should that situation stabilize, the Republicans would lose their most effective weapon. Once Kansas had peacefully entered the Union as a free state under the banner of popular sovereignty, Democrats happily observed, there was no other territory in which similar conflicts might be expected. Slavery, everyone seemed to agree, had no chance in Oregon, Nebraska, Minnesota, Washington, Utah, or New Mexico. The territorial issue that had torn at the country since 1820 might finally have a chance to die down. When it did, moderates on both sides hoped, reason would return to American politics.

In his inaugural address, James Buchanan mentioned a case pending before the Supreme Court, the case of Dred Scott, a slave. That case had moved its way through various levels of courts for more than a decade. Scott, born in Virginia around 1800, had in the 1830s been taken by his master, an army surgeon, to the territories of Illinois and Wisconsin, well above the Missouri Compromise line, and then back to St. Louis. In 1846

*James Buchanan
of Franklin County.*

Scott petitioned for his freedom, claiming that his earlier residence in the free territory of Illinois entitled him to free status. Democratic judges and lawyers worked to deny Scott his freedom on the grounds that such a precedent would undermine the right of Southerners to take their slaves, their constitutionally protected property, into the territories. A Republican lawyer agreed to take Scott's case before the Supreme Court to counter the Democrats' aggressive claims. Unfortunately for the Republicans and Scott, five Southern Democrats sat on the court, along with two Northern Democrats, one Northern Whig, and one Northern Republican. Presiding was Chief Justice Roger B. Taney (pronounced "tawney"), an eighty-year-old man first appointed to the court by Andrew Jackson in 1835, well known for his determination to defend slavery at every opportunity.

The *Dred Scott* case came before the Supreme Court during the superheated months of 1856, when Kansas, the Brooks/Sumner affair, and the presidential election commanded the country's attention. Although the case could have been decided on relatively narrow grounds, the Democratic members of the Court wanted to issue a sweeping pronouncement that would settle once and for all the question of slavery in the territories. President-elect Buchanan pressured a fellow Pennsylvanian on the Court to side with the Southerners. Two days after Buchanan took office in March 1857, the Court announced its decision in the *Dred Scott* case. It took Chief Justice Taney two hours to read the opinion. What he read shook the nation.

Taney spent half his time denying that Scott had the right to bring a case in the first place. Black people, Taney decreed, could not become citizens of the United States or exercise the rights of citizenship because "they were not included, and were not

Richard Taney at the time of the Dred Scott *decision.*

intended to be included, under the word 'citizens' in the Constitution." In chilling language and with distorted history, Taney
declared that at the time the Constitution was written, throughout the "civilized and enlightened portions of the world," members of the "negro African race" were held to be "altogether unfit
to associate with the white race . . . and so far inferior, that they
had no rights which the white man was bound to respect; and
. . . might justly and lawfully be reduced to slavery for his bene-

fit." Therefore, Dred Scott had never been a citizen of Missouri and had no right to bring suit. Taney also decreed that Congress had never held a constitutional right to restrict slavery in the territories and that, therefore, the Missouri Compromise of 1820 was invalid. Two justices dissented from the majority's opinion, but the decision stood as the law of the land. In the meantime, a descendant of Dred Scott's original owner bought the slave and set him free; Scott died the next year.

White Southerners exulted that they had been vindicated by the *Dred Scott* decision, that the Supreme Court was on their side, that the Republicans' demand for territories free of slavery was simply unconstitutional. The Republicans, however, sneered at the decision, which they saw not as the pronouncement of a disinterested group of justices but rather as one more corrupt act by the Slave Power conspiracy. A New York newspaper held that the Court's decision was "entitled to just so much moral weight as would be the judgment of a majority of those congregated in any Washington barroom." The Republicans reprinted the dissenting opinions in the *Dred Scott* case and denounced the decision in the state legislatures they controlled throughout the North. They argued that the Founding Fathers had never intended slavery to be a permanent part of the United States, that the founders had carefully avoided using the word *slavery* in the Constitution and merely tolerated slavery because they expected it to wither away on its own. If the *Dred Scott* decision were followed to its logical conclusion, these northern Republicans warned, the United States would reopen the slave trade with Africa and even extend slavery into Northern states, where it had been banned.

The Democrats, for their part, argued that the Republicans' response to the Supreme Court's decision showed just how dangerous they really were. The Franklin newspaper vented its rage, "denouncing the manner in which the Black Republican press speak of the Supreme Court. Its members are pronounced to be 'scoundrels;' its decisions are declared to be 'of no more weight than would be the judgment of a majority in a Washington bar-room;' it has done a Benedict Arnold work; and its proper authority is gone beyond recovery. And this is said of a tribunal . . . which the Constitution of our country expressly says shall extend to cases of law and equity under it and laws passed in pur-suance of it." In the eyes of the Democrats, the Republicans were the lawless ones, the ones who would overthrow the nation for political gain, using slavery for their own partisan purposes.

SLAVERY had never been stronger in the United States than it was in 1857. The four million slaves of the South extended over a vast territory, stretching from Maryland to Texas. Four hundred thou-sand slaveowners had two billion dollars invested in their human property. Theorists devised ever more elaborate and aggressive defenses of slavery, no longer arguing that it was merely a neces-sary evil or an unfortunate inheritance from the English or a bur-den that had to be shouldered with Christian forbearance, but rather an instrument of God's will. Slavery, its defenders argued, when seen from the largest perspective, was a progressive force in the world, a means of civilizing and Christianizing Africans otherwise lost to barbarism and heathenism. Southern physicians went to great lengths to prove that Africans and their descen-dants were physically and intellectually inferior to whites, dependent on white guidance for their very survival.

Some defenders of slavery argued that slavery was *better* than free labor, more humane and Christian. If the hypocritical and self-righteous men of the North would admit it, white Southerners argued, free labor exacted a great cost. Men, women, and children went hungry when unemployment, ill health, or old age struck because no one in the North felt any responsibility for

THE VIRGINIA HOUSEKEEPER.

White and black women worked together in slavery and in freedom.

anyone else. In the South, by contrast, theorists such as George Fitzhugh of Virginia insisted, slaveholders cared for their slaves even when those slaves had grown too old or feeble to work. The South's relative lack of schools, orphanages, asylums, and prisons, the defenders of the region insisted, was evidence not of a backward society but of a personalized society where individual responsibility replaced impersonal institutions. Compare the status of free blacks in the North and the South, white Southerners challenged, and you will find that white Northerners showed much less concern for the black people who lived in their own communities than they did for slaves they never saw. Augusta County's newspaper bragged that the number of slaves had increased in the 1850s, showing that Virginia's Shenandoah Valley was not being drained of these valuable people.

DESPITE their public agreement on the justice, even necessity, of slavery, important political differences divided Southerners. At one extreme were the so-called fire-eaters, virulent defenders of the South and slavery. These men, more often editors than office holders, more often young than old, saw themselves as the voice of honesty. Fire-eaters such as Robert Barnwell Rhett and Edmund Ruffin argued that the abolitionists and their Republican supporters intended to destroy the South. The only sane response, they believed, was to face the issue squarely and aggressively, to agitate the slavery issue constantly, to refuse to yield an inch in the territories or anywhere else. The fire-eaters were calling for secession as early as 1857.

At the other end of the political spectrum in the South were the former Whigs and Know Nothings. They considered the

Edmund Ruffin, a leading Southern secessionist from Virginia.

Democrats, especially the fire-eaters, great threats to the future of the South and slavery. The Democrats' relentless calls for Southern rights and the expansion of slavery, they argued, did as much as the abolitionists to inflame Northern sentiment against the South. Former leaders of the Whigs and Know Nothings did their best to pull their allies into a new party opposed to the Democrats and attractive to a "thoughtful, sedate, constitution-abiding, conservative class of men." Unionists, of which there were many in the South—especially in the upper South and in cities, but also in some of the richest plantation districts—felt drawn to this position. The editors of the former Whig and American newspapers chided the Democrats for continually agitating the slavery question. Augusta County was dominated by the more moderate men, but contained vocal and visible advocates of Southern rights as well. The *Staunton Spectator* took a steady Unionist position, while the *Vindicator* spoke in hotter language.

The northern Democrats felt enormous pressure from the South, both from their allies and from their opponents. Southern Democrats kept at Buchanan, Douglas, and other Northern Democrats to take strong pro-Southern positions, even if those positions eroded Democrats' support in the North. Southern votes, they argued, had given Buchanan his margin of victory. The Democratic *Valley Spirit* in Franklin County agreed with this assessment of the situation and seldom let an opportunity pass to speak for the South. In 1858, that paper ran an announcement that read: "People of Franklin County! Turn from the Scheming Demagogues who are trying to prejudice you against your Southern brethren, and listen to the voice of . . . prominent and patriotic citizens of your county, who as long as twenty one years ago published to the world their condemnation of the assaults of Abolitionists upon the institutions of the South—assaults now repeated, more violently than ever, by the Black Republicans of Pennsylvania and of all the Northern States." The paper then reprinted a report on an anti-abolitionist meeting in Franklin in 1837, which had attracted some of the most prominent men in the county.

By the late 1850s, the abolitionists had become both firmly entrenched and somewhat discouraged. They had succeeded in making slavery widely detested throughout the North and had created much of the anti-Southern energy that flowed into the Republican Party. But abolitionists distrusted that party. The Republicans seemed interested only in the welfare of the white North, in keeping the territories open to Northern men. Republicans explicitly denied any intention of ending slavery in the South, the very reason the abolitionists had come into being over a quarter of a century before. The Republicans were certainly preferable to the pro-Southern Democrats, abolitionists believed, but that still left plenty of room for dissatisfaction and distrust.

Within the Republican Party itself, men sharply differed among themselves over the proper course of action against the South. Some urged an aggressive posture, while others cautioned that more defensive tactics were safer and more effective in the long run. Some were former Whigs who had always distrusted the Democrats, while others were Democrats who had only recently become disgusted over the events in Kansas. Some wanted to have nothing whatsoever to do with black Americans, fearing that to appear soft on the race issue was to lend credence to charges of the Democrats that they were abolitionists in dis-

Abolitionists led rousing meetings throughout the North.

guise. Other Republicans insisted that blacks in the North be treated, as one of them put it, "something like human beings" and given a chance to earn a living.

PEOPLE saw the Illinois senate election of 1858 as a litmus test of national opinion and strategy. Abraham Lincoln, though possessing considerable political assets, was still very much the underdog against the most prominent Democrat in the country other than President Buchanan—Stephen Douglas. As a Whig in a heavily Democratic state, Lincoln had not found it easy to win or hold office in the 1840s and 1850s. Lincoln's modest beginnings on the Kentucky and Illinois frontier, where he received only one year of formal education, lay comfortably in the past. Still, he longed for a major public office.

Though the short, portly, well-established Stephen Douglas seemed the opposite of Abraham Lin-
coln, the two men in fact shared a great deal. Douglas, too, had grown up poor and Douglas, too, had made himself into what he had become by the late 1850s. Douglas, although the most prominent Democrat in the country, was actually four years younger than Lin-

Abraham Lincoln in 1860.

coln, who had watched Douglas with some envy and jealousy over the preceding two decades. Both Lincoln and Douglas identified quite easily with the voters of Illinois, sharing their constituents' moderate positions on most national issues.

Senator Douglas, though reluctant to give the relatively unknown Lincoln a share of attention, finally agreed to hold seven joint debates in the late summer and early fall. The candidates would take turns opening and closing the debates, with every word transcribed by reporters from across the country. Each candidate sought above all to persuade the audience that he was the safer and more consistent man. Douglas sought to tar Lincoln with the brush of abolitionism, while Lincoln sought to portray Douglas as the tool of the slaveholding South.

Let the sovereign white people of each state decide for themselves, in the fullness of time, Douglas counseled, whether they would have slavery or not. Lincoln charged that Douglas's strategy merely postponed an inevitable reckoning between the slave states and the free states. He argued that "a house divided against itself cannot stand. . . . Either the opponents of slavery will arrest the further spread of it, and place it where the public mind shall rest in the belief that it is in the course of ultimate extinction, or its advocates will push it forward till it shall become alike lawful in all the States, old as well as new, North as well as South." Notwithstanding Douglas's efforts to dismiss the morality of slavery as beside the point in a senatorial campaign, that morality repeatedly surfaced in the debates. Lincoln argued that *he*, not Douglas, was the one defending true self-government. Douglas's policy permitted the forces of slavery to grow stronger and more aggressive, while Lincoln's would place slavery on the path toward "ultimate extinction." It would likely be several generations before that extinction occurred, Lincoln believed, and it would probably need to be accompanied by the colonization of the former slaves out of the United States, but the process could begin in 1858.

Lincoln had to balance carefully on the issue of African Americans.

The Republican paper in Franklin County showered praise on Lincoln and quoted him at length. Lincoln claimed the heritage of the Founding Fathers: "Wise statesmen as they were, they knew the tendency of prosperity to breed tyrants, and so they established these great self-evident truths, that when in the distant future some man, some faction, some interest, should set up the doctrine that none but rich men, or none but white men, or none but Anglo-Saxon white men, were entitled to life, liberty, and the pursuit of happiness, their posterity might look up again to the Declaration of Independence, and take courage to renew the battle which their fathers began." Lincoln did not believe in intellectual or social equality between blacks and whites and would not grant black men the right to intermarry with whites, serve on juries, or vote; but he did believe that black men had the right not to be slaves. The election was close, with Douglas remaining the senator from Illinois, but Abraham Lincoln had won as well. He had become nationally famous, identified as the spokesman for a principled yet restrained antislavery.

TENSIONS between the North and South usually cooled after elections had passed and the bonds of business, family, and nation reasserted themselves. Politicians in both the North and the South knew that many people thought politicians enflamed sectional animosity for their own selfish ends. But the political environment did not have a chance to calm in 1859, for it was then that John Brown returned to the national scene.

John Brown had become famous in the three years since he had burst into prominence in Bleeding Kansas. Antislavery people back East, assured by journalists and even playwrights that

Brown had not personally killed anyone at Pottawatomie, admired the hard man for his confrontational opposition to slaveholders. He actually acted on what other antislavery people only talked about. Thus, as he toured New England in search of funds to carry on the cause, he found willing listeners and open pockets. Antislavery folk were eager to contribute to the fight against slavery in Kansas, not realizing they were contributing to a fight against slavery much closer to home.

Throughout 1857 and 1858 Brown planned a raid on the federal arsenal at Harper's Ferry, Virginia, in hopes of arming slaves and launching a revolt. He set up a household in Franklin County under an assumed name and made preparations. Brown tried to win the support of Frederick Douglass when the great African-American abolitionist visited Chambersburg to speak; although Douglass was sympathetic, he thought the plan doomed logistically. But Brown pressed on. One of his lieutenants moved to Harper's Ferry and even established a family there, prepar-

Harpers Ferry, Virginia.

ing the way for the attack. The assault on Harper's Ferry began in earnest in the summer of 1859, when Brown rented a farm seven miles away and began assembling his men and munitions. To his disappointment, he could recruit only twenty-one men, five

of them African Americans. Brown's sons accounted for three of the number, while runaway slaves, free blacks, abolitionist editors, and college students made up the rest. Most of them were quite young, in their twenties.

The raid began easily enough on Sunday, October 16, as Brown's men quickly seized the arsenal and a rifle-manufacturing plant. Rather than merely taking the weapons and freeing local slaves, however, Brown and his men occupied the small armory building and waited for word to spread

Harpers Weekly depicted the events at Harpers Ferry in great detail to an audience hungry for news of events there.

among the slaves of Virginia that their day of liberation had come. The word spread instead, though, among local whites, who quickly surrounded the armory and Brown's men, killing or capturing eight of them. Militia from Virginia and Maryland arrived the next day, followed soon after by federal troops under the command of Robert E. Lee and J. E. B. Stuart. The troops rushed

the armory, easily overwhelming Brown's men. Ten of the abolitionist forces were killed, five (including Brown) wounded, and seven escaped to Canada or the North. Brown was tried within two weeks and found guilty. He was sentenced to be hanged exactly a month later, on December 2. While he was awaiting execution, a rumor spread throughout Virginia that Northern men were coming to rescue him. Eager to do their part, forty-seven Augusta men grabbed a train to Charlestown to put down the rescue effort, only to discover the call a false alarm. A Staunton paper had to admit that the episode bore "a ludicrous

The Trial of John Brown.

John Brown at the time of Harpers Ferry.

aspect," but few people were laughing at the Brown raid or its response as a whole.

The entire event, from the raid to Brown's execution, took only about six weeks to unfold. Yet those six weeks in late 1859 saw opinion in both the North and the South change rapidly. Contradictory reports and rumors eventually settled into an accepted narrative of events. Public opinion in the North and South, mixed at first, crystallized into sharply opposing viewpoints. Even those Northerners who were appalled at the violence were also appalled at the speed with which Brown was tried and condemned. Even those Southerners who read with reassurance early denunciations of Brown in the North were appalled when they realized that many Northerners refused to condemn the raid and even applauded it.

The *Staunton Spectator* assured Northerners that "while the crazy fanatics of the North imagine that the poor negro, smarting under a galling sense of his degradation, and inspired by a noble impulse of resistance to tyranny, is ready at a moment's warning to grasp the murderous pike and fight for his freedom, the people of the South feel the most perfect security in the full assurance that they possess not only the willing obedience but the strong attachment of their slaves." The *Staunton Vindicator* pointed out that even the bitter political divisions among the residents of Augusta County faded in the face of John Brown's raid. "The people of Virginia are divided by no party lines in reference to the late outrage against its sovereignty; and . . . the conservatives and patriots of all parties unite in denouncing it, and recommending preparation for the prevention or resenting of like outrages."

In Franklin County, the Southern-sympathizing *Valley Spirit* expressed embarrassment that "Our community has by some means, of which we were entirely unaware, become mixed up with this insurrection. While we were harbouring, for months these desperadoes among us we do not believe that a single one of our white citizens was in any way connected with them, or even suspected their designs. In regard to our blacks it is believed that a portion of them knew the object of these men, were associated with them, and would have joined them if successful. There is no sympathy in this community for the fugitives, and if any of them should come this way they will receive no assistance or protection from any of our citizens." The Republican *Repository* found itself in a more awkward situation, since the Democrats blamed Brown's raid on the Republicans and "our Southern neighbors of Maryland and Virginia, bordering on Pennsylvania, are very indignant at the citizens of Chambersburg— regarding them as the most fanatical 'abolitionists' with which the country is troubled." In an example of the heated language that began to fly in the wake of Brown's raid, the *Repository* lashed out at the South. "The citizens of Chambersburg are an order-loving, law-abiding people, and in these respects, or in any other moral virtue that goes to make good American citizens and lovers of the Union, are the superiors of our 'Southern brethren' located on the 'border' or in any other part of 'Niggerdom.' "

The Democrats met in Charleston in April 1860, to decide on their presidential nominee for the fall election. As expected, the Northern Democrats supported Stephen Douglas and popular sovereignty, which they offered as a compromise with the South. But Southern Democrats, outraged at the Northern response to Dred Scott, Kansas, and John Brown, demanded that the party explicitly support the rights of slaveholders to take their slaves into the territories. Northern Democrats, already besieged by the Republicans in the North, could not afford to make that concession and still have a chance to win. The Southerners proved heedless of this plea, however, and walked out of the convention. Several weeks later, the Northerners met in Baltimore and nominated Douglas; the Southerners, meeting in Charleston, nominated John C. Breckinridge of Kentucky.

Before the two Democratic conventions met again, Unionists in both the North and the South tried to avert catastrophe by nominating a compromise candidate, a candidate who would strictly follow the constitution as it was interpreted by the Supreme Court. Calling themselves the Constitutional Union Party, they settled on John Bell of Tennessee. Many of these Unionists were former Whigs who no longer had a political home. They counted on the other candidates to create a deadlock that would have to be settled in the House of Representatives. There, the Unionists hoped, cooler heads would prevail and legislators would gratefully turn to their compromise candidate.

Between the first Democratic convention and its successors, the Republicans met in Chicago. There, in efforts to put southern concerns at rest, the Republicans denounced the John Brown attack on Harper's Ferry and announced their belief in the right of each state to decide for itself whether it would have slavery. The Republicans cemented their appeal to voters unconcerned with the slavery issue by calling for protective tariffs, internal improvements, and free homesteads for anyone—even those who were not yet citizens—who would settle the West. The Republicans were much stronger than they had been only four years earlier in their first presidential campaign. Party strategists calculated that they need only win Pennsylvania and one other state they had lost to the Democrats in 1856 to wrap up the election. The states they needed to take were Illinois, Indiana, or New Jersey—all of them on the border with the South and all of them far more moderate on the slavery question than states farther north. Thus the Republicans, after tumultuous struggle, turned to a moderate who had recently come to the nation's attention and who was a native son of one of the crucial states: Abraham Lincoln of Illinois.

A certain air of unreality surrounded the election of 1860. People did not know that the way that they voted would bring on a civil war, or even secession. While Stephen Douglas constantly warned of such a danger, both Breckinridge and Lincoln downplayed any such dire consequence, insisting, and believing, that the other side was bluffing. Ironically, all the years of conflict, all the series of crises and near-crises, had persuaded both the North and the South that the other talked tougher than it would act. The parties, especially the Republicans, staged loud and raucous political events that proved long on emotion and short on

OPPOSITE. An election poster for Abraham Lincoln in 1860.

HON. ABRAHAM LINCOLN, OF ILLINOIS.

HON. HANNIBAL HAMLIN, OF MAINE,

FOR PRESIDENT,

FOR VICE PRESIDENT.

PUBLISHED BY CURRIER & IVES,

THE REPUBLICAN BANNER FOR 1860.

clearly defined positions. Lincoln said nothing and stayed close to home while his party leaders displayed fence rails and touted his honesty.

Northerners and Southerners were willing to believe the worst of each other because the election of 1860 was actually two separate elections, one in the North and one in the South. Lincoln made no attempt to explain himself to the South; Breckinridge made little attempt in the North. They never met face to face, either in cooperation or in debate. Bell spoke mainly to the already converted. Douglas, speaking from New England to Alabama and everywhere in between, tried to warn people what could happen if they voted along sectional lines, but few were willing to believe their opponents would have the nerve to act on their threats.

On election day—November 6—Lincoln won in every Northern state except New Jersey. Even though he won only in the North, the election was not even close in the electoral college. Douglas took only Missouri, and that barely. Breckinridge won all the South except the border states of Virginia, Tennessee, and Kentucky, which went with Bell. Even at this late stage of sectional division, though, voters did not fit into easy categories. It was hardly a contest between a rural South and an industrial urban North, for Northern cities tended to vote for compromise candidates, not for Lincoln. Similarly, over half of Southerners voted for Bell or Douglas, supporting the Union over the South.

The election of 1860 revealed the fault lines in both Augusta and Franklin. More than three thousand people came to hear Stephen Douglas in Staunton, but when the election results came in, Bell, the Unionist candidate, dominated in Augusta. He received 2553 votes, Douglas 1094, and Breckinridge, the strong

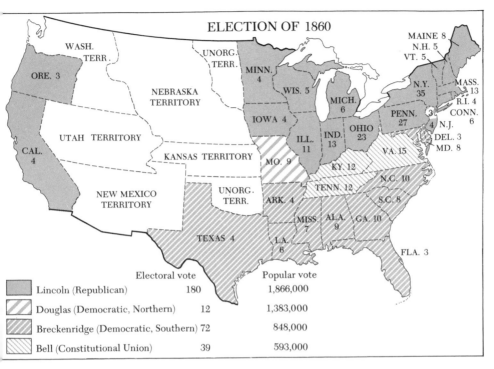

The four-way election of 1860.

Southern-rights candidate, only 218. In Franklin County, by contrast, voters tended to support one of the two extremes: Lincoln or Breckinridge. Lincoln won 4151 votes and Breckinridge 2515. The two moderate candidates fell far behind.

The papers of the two counties tried to gain their bearings in the wake of Lincoln's election. The Democrats' *Staunton Vindicator* made no effort to hide its fear—or its blame of the Southern fire-eaters. "The fight is over, and the victory achieved by the opposition to the South. Lincoln is elected President through the madness and the folly of the South herself; and it now remains to be seen whether or not the councils of prudence, conservatism and right will sway the minds of the people, or rush with blind indifference into all the horrors and griefs of internecine warfare." The staunchly unionist *Spectator* tried to take a more optimistic point of view, even though it lamented that the North had elevated "sectionalism" over the more national perspective of Southerners who had voted for Bell or even Douglas. "Though we are mortified at the success of the Black Republicans in the Presidential election, yet we are rejoiced to know that the elections for Congressmen have resulted in giving us a very safe and decided majority against the Republicans in Congress. The success of the Republicans in the Presidential election is but a barren victory, and its fruits, like the apples of the Dead Sea, will turn to ashes upon their lips." Like its rival Staunton paper, the *Spectator* argued that "The danger is in secession. . . . To secede when there can be no danger would be adding cowardice to treason. To give up when we have the game in our own hands would be cowardly, foolish and criminal." Most white men in Staunton, it appeared, hated the Northern Republicans and feared the Southern secessionists.

In Franklin County, the Democratic *Valley Spirit* also put on a brave face, appealing to nearby Virginia to save the country from war. "We do not yet despair of the Union. There is encouragement in the attitude of Virginia, that ancient and glorious commonwealth, which never loses sight of true principles and never swerves from the path of patriotism. Virginia, whilst firmly maintaining the constitutional rights of the section to which she belongs, will, we are told, remain in the Union and act as mediator between the North and the seceding Southern States." The paper quietly concluded that "the quarrel has gone on too long already. Let the two sections sit down calmly together and talk over the points in issue, and if agreement is out of the question, let them peaceably separate. We do not believe that it is impossible for them to agree." Events soon proved otherwise.

The nation's eyes turned to South Carolina. Influential men there, after all, had talked of secession since the Nullification Crisis nearly thirty years earlier. South Carolinians remembered that they had lost that struggle, however, and did not want to act alone again. Therefore, the South Carolina legislature met on the day after Lincoln's election but did not secede immediately. Its members called for an election two months later to select delegates who would then decide the course the state should follow. In the meantime, they hoped, support for secession would grow and other Southern states would join South Carolina in leaving the Union. Carolinians believed that the states' rights position was unassailable, that the Northern states would be unwilling and unable to resist the Southern states' combined declaration of their individual sovereignty. One South Carolina lawmaker, scoffing at the idea that the North would offer military resistance, laughingly offered to drink all the blood shed over secession.

Deep South states quickly lined up behind South Carolina as secession rallies erupted across the region. Carolina leaders seceded even earlier than they had originally planned, on December 20. By February 1, 1861, Mississippi, Florida, Alabama, Georgia, Louisiana, and Texas had joined the secession movement. On February 9, delegates from these states met in Montgomery, Alabama, and created a provisional constitution, similar to that of the United States except in its explicit guarantee of slavery and states' rights. On February 18, the convention inaugurated a provisional president, Jefferson Davis of Mississip-

Jefferson Davis

pi, and vice president, Alexander H. Stephens of Georgia. Davis, long a national figure, was seen as a moderate, a strong states' rights advocate but not a fervent secessionist.

Many thousands of white Southerners, some of them quite powerful and influential, resisted secession. Some argued that secession was treason. Some warned that the South was committing suicide. Others argued that slavery would be far safer within the Union than in a fragile new country bordered by an antagonistic United States. Other opponents to immediate secession, portraying themselves not as unionists but as "cooperationists," argued that the Southern states should wait until they could cooperate with one another more formally and fully. By presenting a united front to the North, they insisted, the South would not need to secede at all. The North would recognize that the South really meant business this time and would grant the South concessions protecting slavery forever.

Together, these arguments against immediate secession appealed to a large number of Southerners. Even in the Deep South states that rushed to secede in January 1861, almost half of all voters cast ballots for delegates who had not supported immediate secession. The opposition to secession proved stronger still in the upper South, in Virginia, North Carolina, and Tennessee. Under the name of Douglas Democrats, Constitutional Unionists, or simply the Opposition, men of moderate impulse in the upper South mobilized to resist immediate secession. These upper South moderates warned that their states would bear the brunt of any conflict between the lower South and the North, whatever form that conflict might take. And voters listened: more than a month after the first seven states seceded, secession lost in Virginia by a two-to-one margin. The secessionists were stymied, too, in Tennessee, North Carolina, and Arkansas. The leaders of these border states believed they could bargain between the Gulf Confederacy and the North,

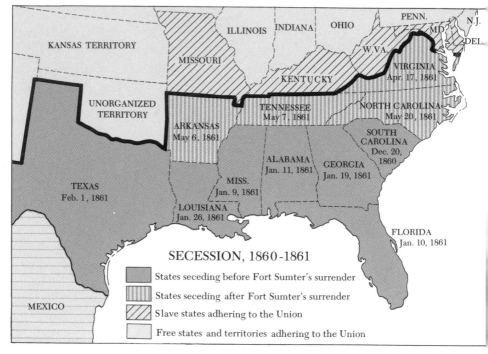

Secession took months to unfold.

winning the concessions the South wanted while maintaining the Union.

Northerners, too, remained quite divided at the beginning of 1861. Many recent immigrants from Ireland and Germany viewed the conflict between the North and the South as none of their business. Northern Democrats bristled at Lincoln's election and his policies. They called for conciliation with the South, for a quieting of the rhetoric. The Franklin *Valley Spirit*, so sanguine of compromise a few months earlier, asked "Is the country to be subjected to the horrors of civil war? We hardly see how the calamity can be averted as things are going. South Carolina is going out of the Union, and all or nearly all the other Southern States will in time follow her, if the Northern States do not repeal their aggressive laws." A week later, with the Confederacy forming, the Democrat paper fumed at their Republican neighbors: "The Democratic party maintain that our government was formed by white men to be controlled by white men for the prosperity and happiness of their race. The Republican party contend that the negro is entitled to equality with the white man—that he must be included and recognized in all our institutions, and have a vote and voice in all our state and national affairs. . . . Must we lose our own freedom in an attempt to free the negro? . . . Northern fanaticism rules the hour—sectional hate and abolition rage have goaded the South to that point where forbearance ceases to be a virtue, and impel them to demand that they be allowed peaceably to withdraw from a confederacy in which they have the equality or safety." Southerners could not have put it better themselves.

Most Republicans, including Lincoln, viewed the rhetoric and even the votes for Southern secession as negotiating stratagems rather than as actual steps toward dissolving the Union. The Republicans showed no propensity to bargain with the South over what remained the key question: federal support for slavery in the territories. The tensions that had built up in the 1850s, Lincoln thought, could no longer be avoided. There had to be some sort of conflict and resolution before the nation could move forward. "The tug has to come," he argued, "and better now, than any time hereafter." If the North postponed action, Lincoln and other Republicans thought, the South would step up its efforts to gain new slave territories in the Caribbean and Central America, dragging the United States into war and perpetuating human bondage far into the future. Like the secessionists, Lincoln did not think the "tug" between North and South would require bloodshed, certainly nothing like the war that soon engulfed the nation.

While Americans fixed their attention on their state and federal capitals in the winter of 1860–1861, the center of the conflict gradually shifted to two obscure forts in the harbor of Charleston, South Carolina. A Kentucky-born U.S. Army officer, Major Robert Anderson, worried that secessionists would attack his small federal force at Fort Moultrie in Charleston and force him either to surrender or to fire on American citizens. Determined to avoid a war, on December 26, 1860, Anderson spiked the guns in Fort Moultrie and moved his small garrison to Fort Sumter, a facility that was still under construction but that occupied a safer position in the center of the Charleston harbor. Anderson hoped that his strategic retreat would prevent an attack on the federal fort. When South Carolina guns drove away a ship President Buchanan had sent with supplies for Anderson and his men, Buchanan chose not to force the issue; like the rest of the nation, he would wait for Lincoln's inaugural on March 4. Meanwhile, South Carolina troops strengthened their position around the Charleston harbor. Anderson's food reserves began to run dangerously low.

Men from both the North and the South worked frantically, but fruitlessly, to find a compromise during these weeks. Some urged the passage of a new constitutional amendment that would permit slavery forever; some urged the purchase of Cuba; some urged that war be declared against another country to pull the United States together again. All the compromises were designed to placate the South, to draw it back into the Union with guarantees of its safety. Abolitionists viewed such maneuvering with disgust and told their countrymen to let the South go, purifying the country and hastening the end of slavery in the process. "If the Union can only be maintained by new concessions to the slaveholders," Frederick Douglass argued, "if it can only be stuck together and held together by a new drain on the negro's blood, then . . . . let the Union perish." Such views were not popular. Mobs blamed the abolitionists for the South's secession and attacked the reformers throughout the North.

On February 11, Abraham Lincoln began a long and circuitous railway trip from Illinois to Washington, pausing frequently along the way to speak to well-wishers. At first, he played down the threat of secession— "Let it alone," he counseled, "and it will go down of itself." But as the train rolled on and the Confederate convention in Montgomery completed its provisional government, Lincoln became more wary. Warned of attempts on his life, Lincoln slipped into Washington under cover of darkness.

Lincoln delivered a somber speech at his inauguration. As sharpshooters stood on nearby rooftops to watch for assassins, Lincoln told the South that he had no intention of disturbing slavery where it was already established, that he would not invade the region, that there would be no shedding of blood, that he would not attempt to fill offices with men repugnant to local sensibilities. But he also warned that secession was illegal, "the essence of anarchy." It was his duty to maintain the integrity of the federal government, and to do so he had to "hold, occupy, and possess" federal property in the states of the Confederacy, including Fort Sumter. Lincoln pleaded with his countrymen to move slowly, to take their time, to let passions cool. "We must not be enemies. Though passion may have strained it, it must not

The United States Capitol at the time of Lincoln's arrival.

break our bonds of affection. The mystic chords of memory, stretching from every battlefield, and patriot grave, to every living heart and hearthstone, all over this broad land, will yet swell the chorus of the Union, when again touched, as surely they will be, by the better angels of our nature."

People heard in Lincoln's inaugural what they chose to hear. Republicans and Unionists in the South thought it a potent mixture of firmness and generosity. Skeptics in the North, South, and Europe, on the other hand, focused on the threat of coercion at Fort Sumter. If Lincoln attempted to use force of any kind, they warned, war would be the inevitable result. Lincoln did not plan on war; he was trying to buy time, hoping that southern Unionists could gather their strength and that compromisers in Washington would come up with a workable strategy.

But there was less time than Lincoln realized. On the very day after Lincoln's speech, Major Anderson reported to Washington that he would be out of food within four to six weeks and that it would take at least twenty thousand troops to resupply the fort. After weeks of listening to various counselors, Lincoln finally decided that he had to act: he would send provisions but not military supplies to Fort Sumter. By doing so, Lincoln would maintain the balance he promised in his inaugural speech, keeping the fort but not using coercion unless attacked first.

The president recognized that this distinction would not matter to the Confederacy. Jefferson Davis and his government, goaded by impatient editors and would-be soldiers, had decided a week earlier that any attempt to reprovision the fort would be in and of itself an act of war, a violation of the territorial integrity of the Confederacy. Davis recognized that no foreign power would take seriously a country, especially one as new and tenuous as the Confederate States of America, if it allowed one of its major ports to be occupied by another country.

The Confederate government decided that their commander in Charleston, P. G. T. Beauregard, should attack Fort Sumter before the relief expedition had a chance to arrive. On April 12, at 4:30 in the morning, Beauregard (ironically, a former student of Major Anderson's at West Point) opened fire on the Union garrison. The shelling continued for thirty-three hours. Anderson

A scene in Charleston as Fort Sumter came under fire.

held out for as long as he could, but when fire tore through the barracks and his ammunition ran low he decided the time for surrender had come. Although no one on either side died in the battle, Northerners, even those who had little faith in their new president or his policies, agreed that the events in South Carolina could not go unanswered. Southerners, even those who resented South Carolina for precipitating the war, agreed that they would have no choice but to come to that state's aid if the North raised a hand against their fellow Southerners.

IMPORTANT FROM CHARLESTON.

MAJOR ANDERSON TAKEN !

ENTRANCE OBTAINED UNDER A FLAG OF TRUCE

NEW YORKERS IMPLICATED !

GREAT EXCITEMENT.

WHAT WILL THE SOUTHERN CONFEDERACY DO NEXT ?

On the 8th inst., about 12 hours before midnight under cover of a
bright sun, Col. George S. Cook, of the Charleston Photographic Light
Artillery. with a strong force, made his way to Fort Sumter. On being
discovered by the vigilant sentry, he ran up a flag of truce. The gate of
the Fortress being opened, Col. Cook immediately and heroically penetra-
ted to the presence of Maj. Anderson, and levelling a double barrelled
Camera, demanded his unconditional surrender in the name of E. Anthony and the Photographic community.

Seeing that all resistance would be in vain, the Major at once surren-
dered, and was borne in triumph to Charleston, forwarded to New York.
and is now for sale in the shape of exquisite Card Photographs at 25cts.
per copy, by

E. ANTHONY,
501 Broadway.

The Trade can send Orders through their Agent.

Breathless news from South Carolina.

Two days after the Confederate flag went up over Fort Sumter on April 15, President Lincoln declared South Carolina in rebellion against the United States and called for seventy-five thousand militiamen from states North and South to help put the rebellion down. Lincoln could have called up far more troops, for men clamored to serve throughout the North. But the president sought to appear restrained in his response. He still hoped that Unionists in Southern states besides South Carolina would rally to the nation's defense if he showed that he was no extremist. Lincoln also acted cautiously because he had not received the approval of Congress, which would not convene until July.

Lincoln's attempt to blend firmness and conciliation failed. Southern states saw the call to the militia as an act of aggression against South Carolina and state sovereignty. The upper South states replied with defiance to Lincoln's requests for their militia. Virginia seceded two days later. Although many people in Virginia, especially in the mountainous western counties, still clung to hopes of avoiding war, two delegates to every one voted for secession on April 17. These Virginians, like white Southerners of all inclinations and temperaments, refused to permit Northern troops to march through their states to defeat South Carolina. Southerners considered this an invasion by an arrogant central government, the very sort of coercion that had triggered the American Revolution. Recognizing the importance of Virginia's addition to their ranks, the Confederacy immediately voted to move their capital to Richmond in May 1861.

The Staunton *Vindicator* looked at the new Southern Confederacy with pride: with "50,000 well drilled troops; the most gifted and experienced statesmen of the age in charge of its civil departments; a treasury well supplied with funds; and sustained

by the hearts and hands of a united people, the new Confederacy bids fair to become one of the most successful and prosperous
governments on the globe. . . . The idea of this government ever
again uniting with a people whose entire education is enmity and
whose highest ambition is oppression, aggression and outrage, is
simply preposterous." The *Spectator*, which had argued against
secession until the last moment, joined in with great enthusiasm
once the decision had been made. The paper blamed Lincoln.
"While one last effort was being made by the friends of peace the
response came. It was heard at Sumter! It was reiterated in the
proclamation of Abraham Lincoln! It was seen in the preparations made by the Federal Government to coerce the Southern
States! And that response severed the last link that bound the
Union party of Virginia to the United States Government." Only
ten men in Augusta voted against secession. Thousands had
changed their minds over the period of a few months, even
weeks.

As it turned out, the Union and the Confederacy divided
about as evenly as possible. Virginia, Tennessee, North Carolina,
and Arkansas, all of which went into the Confederacy, might well
have decided to remain with the Union; had they done so, the
Confederacy would have had little hope of sustaining a successful war against the North. Those states, the three most populous
in the South among them, accounted for half of all manufacturing and half of all food production in the Confederacy. Maryland,
Kentucky, and Missouri, on the other hand, might well have
joined the Confederacy; had they done so, the Union cause
would have been weakened, perhaps fatally. Kentucky and Missouri, possessing white populations and economic resources
larger than those of any Confederate state except Virginia, occu-

pied crucial positions along the major rivers that led into the South.

LOOKING back, knowing that the war dragged on for four years, the cards seem heavily stacked in the North's favor. The Union, after all, had vastly greater industrial capacity, railroads, canals, food, draft animals, ships, and entrepreneurial talent, all the things a mid-nineteenth-century war required. The Union could also claim four times as many white residents as the South—22 million versus 5.5 million. And while the 3.5 million slaves who lived in the Confederacy were extraordinarily valuable to the South, everyone recognized that the slaves could become equally valuable allies for the North under the exigencies of war.

Since the South acknowledged the North's advantages, many people then and since assumed that the Confederates must have been driven either by irrational rage or by heedless bravery. Neither the Confederates nor the North, however, expected the secession crisis to turn into a full-fledged war, much less a four-year war of attrition and endurance. When Lincoln called for the seventy-five thousand militia he called them for only ninety days' service. When Southern boys and men rushed to enlist for the Confederacy in the spring of 1861, they assumed they would be back home in time to harvest their crops in the autumn. Since both sides believed that the other was bluffing and that their opponents were weak and divided, Northerners and Southerners thought the conflict would likely come to a swift, and peaceful, resolution. In such a struggle, sheer numbers did not seem nearly as important as they became.

The military strategies of both sides were intended to mini-mize actual fighting. The South saw itself as purely on the defen-sive; it would wait for Northern armies to invade and then defeat them with the determination of people defending their own homes and farms. As a Staunton paper put it, "We simply want our own soil relieved from the oppression of the North. We want and mean to have our rights and our liberty, or else honourable graves. We are acting on the defensive exclusively." The North, for its part, counted on what became known as the "anaconda plan," after the snake of that name that slowly squeezed its prey to death. That plan depended on sending two forces down the Mississippi River, one by water and one by land, dividing the South in half. At the same time, the Union navy would seal off the South from outside supplies. The goal, general-in-chief Winfield Scott said, was to "envelop the insurgent states and bring them to terms with less bloodshed than any other plan." Ground troops and land battles would be kept to a minimum.

The Confederacy, from the perspective both of its own strat-egy and that of the North, possessed considerable military advan-tages. It occupied an enormous area, larger than today's United Kingdom, France, Italy, and Spain combined. It possessed dozens of harbors and ports, connected by an excellent system of rivers and an adequate network of railroads. The Confederacy's long border with Mexico made it difficult to seal off outside supplies. The Confederacy could wage a defensive war, drawing on its own resources, fighting on its own land, moving its troops inter-nally from one point to another while the Union had to move around the perimeter. The many country roads of the South, known only to locals, would provide routes for Confederate sur-prise attacks or strategic retreats. Every white Southerner could

Soldiers rushed to have their photos taken in their new uniforms.

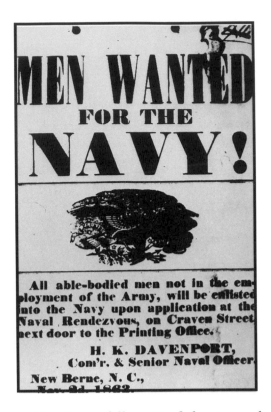

MEN WANTED
FOR THE
NAVY!

All able-bodied men not in the employment of the Army, will be enlisted
into the Navy upon application at the
Naval Rendezvous, on Craven Street
next door to the Printing Office.

H. K. DAVENPORT,
Com'r. & Senior Naval Officer,
New Berne, N. C.,
Nov. 2d, 1862.

be a spy or an ally when a fellow Confederate needed information, food, or medical aid.

The Franklin *Valley Spirit*, which had defended the South for
years, changed its tone when the war began: "A formidable band
of traitors have broken up the Union and made war against the
government. While we considered them friends we battled for
their rights in the Union, but when they determine to break up the
Union and array themselves as enemies against us, we are their
enemies. They are no longer of our household but enemies up in
arms against us. Let us then be up and doing and crush the mon-
ster before it crushes us. Let us be watchful on every side and
allow no man to slumber at his post while the flag of his country is
in danger. Let the watch-word of all be—'READY, AIM, FIRE.' "

Before there could be any firing, however, both sides had an enormous work to do, building armies from little more than rag-tag militia units and enthusiasm. Most of that building took place at the community level, where units formed. Posters went up in Augusta and Franklin just as they went up across the United States in the spring of 1861. A broadside from Staunton proclaimed: "MEN OF VIRGINIA, TO THE RESCUE! Your soil has been invaded by your Abolition foes, and we call upon you to rally at once, and drive them back. We want volunteers to march immediately to Grafton and report for duty. Come one! Come ALL! And render the service due to your State and Country."

And soldiers did come to serve, North and South. Within weeks, hundreds of men from Augusta and Franklin had joined. Some Augusta men traveled to Harper's Ferry, where they found themselves under the command of Thomas Jonathan Jackson, not yet known as "Stonewall." Other Augusta men merely camped on the grounds of the Deaf, Dumb, and Blind Institute in Staunton, awaiting their orders. Others rushed into battle without uniforms, carrying flintlock rifles.

Franklin men followed more orderly recruitment, going to camps rapidly established around the state, one in the county itself. The local paper joked that a supporter sent "some twenty casks of the very superior Lager Beer made at Pittsburg. As an evidence of how gratefully the present was received, the company have resolved to return the casks by the next train empty." Soon, Chambersburg residents claimed to be blasé about the camp. "Our citizens are becoming used to the novelty of the presence of a large body of military in their midst. They seem to attract but little attention, or interest, any longer and our people are settling down to their usual occupations in their quiet way as formerly. The fear of an attack from 'over the line' has also died out, and we would not be much surprised to hear of our young ladies and gentlemen getting up a pic-nic to Harper's Ferry some pleasant day just for the novelty of the thing."

"Ladies" played a large role in these tumultuous days, in ways both ceremonial and practical. Women used their sewing skills, highly cultivated in both the North and the South, to make flags and uniforms. As a Chambersburg paper reported, "a handsome flag was presented to the 7th Regiment, as a mark of regard from the ladies of Chambersburg. The interesting ceremony took place in the Diamond, in the presence of the 7th and 8th regiments and a large concourse of citizens. . . . The whole affair passed off very pleasantly and afforded a high degree of gratification to the soldiers as well as our citizens." In Augusta, the *Vindicator* enthused, "The ladies of Staunton, and especially the pupils of the different Female Institutes here, have entwined their brows with glory-wreaths of evergreen, which beautifully reflect the fresh and buoyant courage of their hearts. For days they have been busily engaged in making the uniforms of the new volunteer companies, scarcely permitting twenty-four hours to pass after the order had been placed in their hands, ere the full uniform, neatly made, was presented to the young soldier. What a touching evidence of the affection of these fair daughters of Virginia and the South for the sunny clime of their nativity. . . . God bless the sweet girls, and God speed and protect the brave boys." Within days of the beginning of the war, women in both communities began to organize hospitals and make supplies.

White people devoted little space in their newspapers or letters to the black people among whom they lived, but both Southerners and Northerners paid attention to expressions of

African-American sentiment in the days of the sectional crisis. For those who cared to notice, the sentiments of Northern blacks were not hard to see. "It is a custom among the colored folks to celebrate the first of August in commemoration of the emancipation of the Slaves in the British West India Islands," a Chambersburg paper noted in 1860. "The colored population of

Clara Barton (1821–1912) oversaw the distribution of vital medicines to Union toops, and later founded the American Red Cross.

this and neighboring towns assembled here, on Wednesday last, and put the day through by a grand pic-nic, military parade, and the other fixens of a jollification in such cases made and provided." They displayed a flag bearing the likeness of Abraham Lincoln. In Augusta, the local paper cheerfully reprinted an article from a Richmond newspaper reassuring whites that black people were proclaiming their eagerness "either to fight under white officers, dig ditches, or any thing that could show their desire to

serve Old Virginia. . . . Such is the spirit among bond and free, throughout the whole of the State. Those who calculate on a different state of things, will soon discover their mistake." Whites wanted to believe that their slaves and employees would stand beside them, that Northern claims of black resentment of slavery were exaggerated, that the Southern people were united across lines of race as well as party.

Many African Americans enlisted on the side of the Union.

ABRAHAM ESSICK, a minister who had traveled within Franklin and neighboring counties throughout the 1850s, confided to his diary on May 8, 1861, that "never did I anticipate such a state of things in my day. Our lot has been cast in calamitous times, and we who are near the confines of slave and free territory will, doubtless, be the greatest suffered. The war spirit aroused in both sections is wonderful. No one could have imagined that the sober-minded Pennsylvanians could be so aroused. Yet it seems that she is taking the lead in furnishing men and means and all the essentials of war. Such unanimity I never heard of. Conservative men, who did all in their power to avert the collision before our flag was dishonored, are now burning with indignation. I have not heard a dissenting voice. From the minister of the gospel through all classes of the community, the senti-

ment is universal, that the government must be sustained, rebellion suppressed and the honor of the nation vindicated."

Sounds of cannon soon echoed through the Valley.

Augusta and Franklin were indeed unified in 1861 in ways they
had never been before. Newspapers that had resisted the drift of
events over the preceding two years declared themselves solidly
behind the war efforts, replacing their calls for compromise with
calls for common purpose against the enemy. Ministers who had
prayed for peace now prayed for victory. Leading men on both
sides who had worked for compromise threw themselves into the
war effort, often becoming officers. Women who had hoped for
conciliation sewed uniforms and made bandages. Young men who
had paid no attention to politics over the last two years proudly
wore uniforms made by their sweethearts. The people on both
sides eagerly awaited battles, certain they would win. The war,
surely, would be short and glorious.

INDEX